Life Through My Eyes

A Poetry Collection

Mishon Moore

Life Through My Eyes

Copyright © 2021 by Mishon Moore

All rights reserved. No part of this book may be reproduced or transmitted in any form or by any means without written permission from the author.

Claire Aldin Publications
P.O. Box 453
Southfield, MI 48037
www.clairealdin.com

ISBN 978-1-954274-01-3 paperback
ISBN 978-1-954274-02-0 eBook

Printed in the United States.

Dedication

This book is dedicated to those who supported me and believed in me. I am grateful to God for His grace and mercy, but ultimately for life itself.

~Mishon

Table of Contents

You Had No Right 9

My Baby Boy 13

Listen 15

In the Beginning 19

This Man 21

Boy, You're My Drug 25

Mind 27

Love Letter 31

Strangers 35

Unloved 39

God, Who Am I? 43

Judge Not 45

Alone 47

The System 49

Black Man 51

I Can't Breathe 55

Unspoken Land 59

It's Hard to Say Goodbye 61

You Had No Right

You had no right
To strip her of her stripes, strip her of her identity
You had no right
To erase her innocence
You had no right
To play her God, control her outcome, path or way
To her destiny

You had no right
To cloud her mind like a spring night
When the blunts are blazing in the air
And you are stuck in a smoke cloud

You had no right
To paint a picture of her
Before she could look in the mirror
And see the woman looking back at her

You had no idea that the day you decided
To explore her curves, caress her bottle shape
And feel her warm blossomed flower

That you would lock her away

In a mental, emotional, spiritual and physical jail

You held her captive with your word

Your disregard of her wants and needs

You had no right

To make her life a scene from Nightmare on Elm Street

You had no right

How could you turn such a beautiful flower

That God took his time to create

And destroy it and turn it into

A garden of dying hope, dying love

Dying trust, dying petals

That fell every time her mind took her back to that day

You striped her of herself

You had no right

To create a beast when God created a beauty

That would grow to be all she could be

But you had no right to interfere, my dear

You had no right

To bring hate in her heart

And thoughts that it was her fault

Like she seeks for you to strip her
Of her courage, her self-esteem
You had no right!

You had no right
To break down what you didn't build
You had no right!

Now she has to cry to God, that He fixes her
You had no right
To bury her six feet under
When you didn't bring her life
With hours of pain and labor

You had no right
To alter God's masterpiece
Look at the picture you painted
How she has to recreate.
You had no right!
The right was hers, not yours

You had no right
To take away her voice, silence her mind
chain her freedom of choice

You had no right!

Now she is struggling to overcome the day you raped her.

9/15/2018

My Baby Boy

I first laid eyes on you and my world changed for the better
I looked into your eyes with so much joy
I can do this because with you I knew
I couldn't do no better

As I held you, listening to you breathe
I felt your little heartbeat and I played with your little feet
God saw fit to bless me with a little baby boy
That tugged at my soul and melted my heart
Nothing or no one could tear us apart
This new journey, you will lead
It's amazing that the seed I planted
blossomed into this beautiful creation from the skies above
God gave you to me to love, protect, teach, guide
And embrace you with his everlasting grace

You're my miracle baby who came in a time of need
Helped my heart not to bleed
Gave me reason to succeed and live again
It was like when Jesus died for my sins and I was born again
When I first laid eyes on you

I knew from that day forward that I had all I needed in life
Your hugs and kisses are like the warmth from a summer sky
I love you baby boy
It's you and I
9/19/2018

Listen

Hello, are you there?

Hello, are you there?

Look at me

I'm talking to you

Don't tune me out just listen

When you look at me

You see my brown skin

My wide, but slim eyes

My crooked smile

My curvy shape with a little pug, my black short straight hair

Hey, listen to me!

Are you there?

After you're done examining me with your judgmental eyes

Your hypocritical mind, your cold heart, your desperate soul

Can you still listen to me?

I am more than what meets the eye

I am courageous

You don't know how many fights I had to fight

I am saved

You don't know how many days I wanted to end

I am an intellectual

You don't know how many times my voice was silenced

Hello, are you there?

Yes, you look at me

I'm talking to you

Love me from the inside out

I have bruises and scars that you can't see

But they made me be me

I have a scar from the time I lashed out

You felt it was unnecessary but what you don't know is

It already happened to me

Smile.

Stop being so mad and angry

You didn't know that day was the day my parents died.

Stop judging me instead ask why

Why such a frown?

Hey are you listening

Look at me now

Do you understand

Not all the time is the outside

What the picture really looks like

When I am happy but I have no energy to project it

It is because you can't see the inside

You didn't know that happiness is what I felt

Hold my hand… you feel that?

My heart is beating through my hand

My hand shaking, but nothing is wrong on the outside

Nothing happened to me but on the inside

My body is having its own silent panic attack

For whatever reason but will you be there

To see me overcome every season

Are you listening?

Look at you

Are you still there?

My body has a mind of its own

But I bet you didn't know that

Because the inside doesn't look like the statue

On the outside visible to your eyes

Watch this

Are you still listening?

What did I say?

Look - don't look at my glass as half empty

Look at my glass as half full

Because its more to me than my outer, you see

9/16/2018

In the Beginning

In the beginning
It was phone calls, text messages, and picture mail
In the beginning
It was I love you, let me hold you, let me console you
In the beginning
Your representative represented you well
Who knew it all would fail
In the beginning
You had me under your spell
Trying to make it invisible so you couldn't tell
In the beginning
There were gifts, cards, candy and even flowers, too
Pop-ups out the blue
In the beginning
Never knew the true you
Failing head over hills in love with you
Singing to you telling you all that was expressed inside of me
In the beginning
Never wanted it to end, nine out ten, you weren't my kin
In the beginning
It was all a fairytale

Thought I hit the jackpot like a car sale

In the beginning

In the beginning

I never saw the end

3/30/2012

This Man

The sensation of his kiss warmed my heart

Like a summer morning bliss

He whispered in my ear 'can I caress…caress your mind?

Let me take my time

Hold on sir, shit, that was deep

What's your goal here?

He replied 'to put yo ass to sleep'

Every word he whispered was slow and sweet

Could this be real or did I fall asleep?

Having a dream of this fairy tale

or is this man really my reality?

Falling in love is my fear

This man got me contemplating my very own existence

This can't be real, not the way he is caressing my mind

He gives me chills up and down my spine

Intellectual, charismatic, enticing, bold and boastful

Need I say more?

This man is the billboard for everlasting romance

He got my mind racing, my body shaking, my soul screaming

Got me contemplating…contemplating what to do with this

Can it be true?

Is this man the dream come true?

Massage my heart with your love

Hold my soul in place

Speak life into me

Help me win this race

Keep my body at a steady pace

Standing there well dressed

Smelling good, business like, mixed with a little hood

Can't stop staring at this man

Looking deep into my eyes

Piercing my soul in place

Speak life into me, help me win this race

Keep my body at a steady pace

Standing there well-dressed smelling good

Business mixed like a little hood

Can't stand staring at this man

Looking deep into my eyes, piercing my soul

His mouth open with a world of confirmation

Affirmation and a helluva lot of stimulation

It's getting hot, he ran his hand across my cheek and said

'Fear not, my beautiful queen

Let me lead you, let me take care of you

Watch what I can do"

I glance up and say take the lead

Let the planet take this seed

Your tender touch is all I need

Holding my hand standing with so much demand

He sweeps me off my feet

My heart begins to skip a beats

This man, this man with a master plan

The heart wants what the heart wants is the saying

The sensation of his kiss

Warmed my heart like a summer morning bliss

10/29/2019

Boy, You're My Drug

Boy, you're my drug

Loving you is like the sunrise kissing the morning sky

Being by your side standing strong, ready for war

Letting nothing or no one infiltrate in the bond we share

My heart skips a beat every time you stare at me

This love is for real, you see

Praying to God daily that He keeps us in perfect peace

Keeping God numero uno

With Him we're the dynamic duo

Boy, you're my drug

But I can't breathe

I can't seem to get enough of your love for me

Your love feels so good, but it has a hold on me

My emotions run deep, high and low; never a steady flow

My mind races at the thought of you,

your name sends chills down my spine

But I can't breathe

Your word sometimes can be so cold with an empty hold

But like the glow of the night moon

I yearn for your warm embrace

Praying God showers us with his grace
I picture the day when I say the words 'I do'
Becomes a lifestyle, a beautiful never-ending journey

Boy, you're my drug
I want to overdose, be comatose
High off your presence, wrapped up in your everlasting essence
But I gotta stay focused
Because you'll make me lose focus
You make my mind like a maze
making you everything I crave
I have to save myself from this hypnotizing love you have over me

Boy, you're my drug
I need you like flowers need the rain
The sky needs the clouds, the earth needs the heavens
When your hand caresses my body like it's your map
To everlasting adventure, take me to your land and let me explore your world
Boy you're my drug
9/19/2018

Mind

Have you ever felt like your thoughts were like
A little person on your shoulder who talks back to you?
Sometimes they are encouraging
But sometimes they are disturbing
The voice that they have is so loud, confusing nonetheless
Very convincing they know what's best for you
So sit there while I do the rest for you

Your thoughts say you got this, oh wait, no you don't
You will lose, you will get defeated, say okay you can win
Stop.. stop!
I can't hear myself think
Stop interrupting me
Ha ha
I am your thoughts
I do your thinking
No, I control you, you don't control me
I'm the headmaster
I see you trying to play me
Oh look at you, you can't even handle you
Do you ever feel that your thoughts try to drown you?

Your thoughts pull you in so many directions

Most of the time they leave you sitting there

Trying to figure out who just robbed you

Robbed you of your stability, robbed you of your peace

Robbed you of your understanding, feeling lost and confused

You have to tell your thoughts you make the rules

Stop and relax tell yourself I got this

I am going to win this fight

I will make the right decisions

Don't let your mind play tricks on you

Have you thinking that you weren't built for this

Have you ever sat quietly and became one within

Detach from the world

And allow your mind, body and soul to be aligned

Many times we go, and go, and go

Like the Energizer bunny

We forget to take time to listen to ourselves

Your thoughts can be encouraging

If you allow nothing but positive thoughts to confine you

Your thoughts can't dictate your outcome

So tell that little person on the inside of you

That you have stuff to do

Tell your thoughts "You can't overpower me!"

I will prevail you watch and see

9/21/2018

Love Letter

This is my love letter to you
The love of my life
We chose to embark on this journey
That would have its highs and lows

This is my love letter to you
The love of my life
Nothing is ever perfect
But what counts the most are the effects
Even on the bad days, I still choose you
I can't lie somedays feel that you have thrown in the towel
But then you seem to find that little bit of love that's left
And you make it count

I get it my love, I really do because I, too have days
When it seems like it's closer to the end
But then I pray to the Lord above
If you see fit, Lord, help us out a little bit
Lord, help us find the love that started our love story

This is my love letter to you

The love of my life

When the days come and it seems

You have no more fight inside

It does something crazy to me

It silences me, it takes me to an empty place

But I'm in it to win this race

Nothing is perfect, my dear

But when love is strong, you can't lose or fold

This is my love letter to you

Just letting you know that on the bad days

That's when my heart still beats for you

I hope you can see that our love is worth

The story that it will tell

We made it after all the rain

We made it to tell it all

Better days are near peeking from behind those dark clouds

That the bad days developed

Here's a bit of sunshine to remind you

Why you are in it after all

This is my love letter to you

The love of my life

Don't give up on something that became a part of you

Yes, some days seem so clear to say

I did my part, I did my very best

But this is something I can't play a part in

Then when God finds it in His plans to bless us one more time

To see the picture of the good times

Remember God had to fight for a relationship with us,

But he never gave up

And daily he stands and gives it His all

I just want to tell you that we got this

Just think about the love that started this

Watch what I say

I'm telling you we got this

This is my love letter to you

The love of my life

Trying to be each other's peace, support and

Encouraging each other will push us further

The love of my life, think twice

Let it settle in, we got this

Let's continue to pray together, praise together,

Build together

Climb to the top together

They say birds of a feather flock together

Let's make this thing forever

I pray God continues to turn things around
More smiles, less frowns
Even on the bad days,
I hope your heart still chooses me to see

This is my love letter
I promise it will be gloomy days
But I'll do my very best, my very best to let my light shine
Promise me that even in the dark times
You will try this love thing one more time

This is my love letter to you
No everything won't be happy
But I'll be there when the sad moments arrive

This is my love letter
Just letting you know the love that started it all
Is still enough
Just take the time to explore it
Let's live our best lives

This is my love letter to you
The love of my life
9/11/2018

Strangers

The sound of my heart beating

Due to the nervousness of my body

The silence that echoes through the room

Nothing to say

Nothing to see

Stop pretending with me

I used to know you

Now I have no clue who you are

A stranger standing right in front of me

Your word is short and not filled with emotions

Instead they are filled with coldness

You don't have to pretend with me

You are free

Indeed the pretending is what hurts the most

More than knowing that you are no longer here with me

I prayed that one day, things would change, get better

Maybe even be able to connect on different levels

But all that happened is that our bodies

Have grown colder and unfamiliar

You can stop pretending with me

I have set you free

Free indeed

No more pretending to care or even be there

Just leave and never look back

This shit is killing me

Walking around with nothing to say

Only sex is left and that's beginning to fade away

Fade away like your heart

Stolen in the darkness of the night

Emotionless has become the norm

No words can form

A blind man can see the distance

Instead of complimenting my body

Compliment me like the others do

Say 'I'm proud of you'

Say 'damn you are doing yo thang'

But instead I get 'let me bang'

Don't be attracted to my physical

But my mental and spiritual

If that ain't on the menu

Then you can leave

Remember you are free

Free indeed you don't have to pretend with me

Heart in a million pieces

I'll get the glue

You watch me I'll bounce back

And I'll be stronger

A guard will greet all who approach

Because this shit killed me

Walk away you stranger

Take your bag

Over time, I won't be sad

I'll be healed

I pray you never have to feel this pain in your heart

Your soul must be strong or you will fold

I got this, no more pretending

Even the sex couldn't change the scene of this horror movie

4/11/2020

Unloved

You don't love her anymore
She can see it in your eyes
It's all lies
Nights grew colder when you weren't next to her
Stop pretending that you love her
It's unfair to both of you
Conversations became foreign
Empty like a gun with no clip

You don't love her anymore
She can see it in your eyes
It's all lies
Your kisses turn invisible like Casper the friendly ghost
Stop playing with her heart like double dutch
One minute you in one minute you out
Your hugs went away like MJ faded away
Your life was an open book but one day it became a secret
An untold story to your biggest fan
But she felt the change in her soul
Tell her you don't love her
Give her strength back

Think back to what made you fall in love with her
Try to feel that
If something is worth it
You will fight for it

Stop pretending that you love her
Tell her the truth, let her in
She doesn't feel safe when your arms are near
Instead, she feels fear
Fear that today isn't the day
He will pretend to love me again
She yearns for your love so the fakeness she erases
She knows that your love is deepened on the day
She accepts this sad love song because she loves you enough
For the both of you
She loves her enough for you

You used to love to engage now you ignore her in rage
You treat her like she doesn't exist
Love her again and you don't have to pretend
It's okay to let her back in
Let her be a part of your world
Don't give her a key and move without letting her know
All she wants is to build with you

Create an empire and a family that keeps God first

But it seems like that isn't something you knew

Loving her is easier because you understand her

And she understands you more

Don't pretend, let her in

She loves you so she begs you to stay and work it out

She is there for you when the world grows old and blue

Give her a chance just as she gave you to love again

You can sit her down and explore her

With your mind, heart and soul

You all have a love tie, don't let it go

9/20/2018

God, Who Am I?

God, who am I?

You say walk by faith and not by sight

But in my vision

I see brokenness, emptiness, bitterness and confusion

Have faith you say, you are free!

Why are you in self-bondage, self-hate, self-destruction?

You can't even function

God, who am I?

You love me even when I am deep in sin

You loved me when I wanted to give in

You whispered quietly in my ear

I'll always get you through

Through the hurt, the pain and the rain

I'll give you peace

I'll heal your heart, renew your soul

I am the great I am

The one that calmed the sea

The great I am that told the storm to cease

God, who am I?

I seek Your understanding

I seek Your light in darkness

As my heart beats fast, my ears are open

And my eyes look to the hills

I hear this sweet voice, you are me, you are my child

My vision, my product, my grace and mercy

My purpose, my testimony, my example

My example that I am the great I am

That will wash away all your sins

I will turn your midnights into days

I get it, Lord, I get it now

I am me, I am a witness, I am the great I am

God, who am I?

I am a stronger me

9/15/2018

Judge Not

He prepares a table in front of me

In the presence of my enemies.

Whoever thought they would bleed the same blood as me?

Jesus died on the cross for me, who are you to judge me?

Jesus gave me a brand new life, you see

He paid my fee on Calvary

My enemies can't win, won't win, because guess what?

We all sin

The Bible says no sin is greater than another

Put your sins down because you can't judge me

Jesus gave me a brand new life you see

He paid my fee on Calvary

The Bible says there will come a time

When families will divide

Luke 15:23 to be exact

Look it up, it's all facts

Fathers against sons

Mothers against daughters

Sons against fathers

Daughters against mothers

Stepkids against stepparents

And stepparents against step kids

We are so quick to say look what the devil did

But it was the great I am that said it in His plan

Stop trying to create your own story

Jesus has already narrated your beginning and end

So don't judge me, just remember

Jesus paid my fee on Calvary to be free

Your enemies aren't always outside

Sometimes you have to look inside

You'll be surprised that they bleed the same blood as you

9/16/2018

Alone

Scared of life

Scared to be alone

The unknown is the scariest part of the journey

Sometimes it takes hold, hold of your mind, even your soul

Fighting battles but never winning the war

Just another day on the battle field

Scared of life

Scared to be alone

We have to live before we die

Don't get caught playing because you can't hide

Heart feeling broken unloved

Soul holding stories untold

Your mind playing tricks on you

Making you think that this is your destination

When actually it's just another life lesson

That comes with a blessin'

How damaged will you be?

After all this learning from life's lessons

Will it leave you broken or will it put the pieces back together?

Sadness or happiness which one will be forever?

Scared of lfe
Scared to be alone
You accept people lies and their half ass loving you
But you have to understand that it's a time that you have to
Love you more than others do

Scared of life
Scared to be alone
Forcing yourself to overlook how no one cares for you
This journey that we call life ends on that day
What will you have?
Will you just have all that hurts inside or will you live
And have healing inside?
Heal yourself, who you lose along the way is meant to be
But losing you is a choice that you took
10/14/2018

The System

The system went from auctions and whips to bars and burials

Free at last, free at last

Are the words Dr. King spoke to us

But we didn't know it had fine print

Locked up mentally and physically is what they meant

We stood on Malcolm X words

By any means necessary

But we still in slavery

Paying commissary and making too many visits

To the cemetery

The system went from auctions and whips to bars and burials

Moms and dads losing their baby boys to the system

Just another black nigga that got out of his place

Where is our 40 acres?

Where is our reciprocity for all the damage they caused?

Coming up empty handed

Just eyes full of tears and hearts full of sorrow

Instead of chains and beating now

They imprison our mind and time

They take the little pride that's inside the system

Isn't made for you the black man
The black woman who looks like me

Like Adam and Eve, we had no chance
We were born into sin cursed by the white man
Never to be looked at for the one to most succeed but the one
That will always have to pay a deed
Black man stand tall
Black man rise, don't fall
Take back your dignity
Take back your manhood
Take back your businesses
Take back the black family

The system went from auctions and whips to bars and burials
United we stand, divided we fall
Fall for anything so stand for something
The system is the man who gives demands
But you can overcome them all
If you just take a stand, black man
10/11/2018

Black Man

Hey black man, hey black man, yes, I'm talking to you

Straighten your back, hold your head up

Stick yo chest out, unball yo fist

You're important, you're strong, and almighty, too

Something like David when he beat Goliath the giant

Hey black man, hey black man, I'm talking to you

Speak loudly and proudly walk with authority

For you are worthy

Worthy of all the riches of glory

Hey black man, hey black man yea, I'm talking to you

Dress to impress; you're equipped with all the tools

For success

Believe in you because I do

Love how that charisma drips off of you

Hey black man, hey black man, yea, I'm talking to you

You have many duties…

You're a father, brother and a son, too

Well, you get the picture

How essential your presence is on this earth

Make your mark black man, I'm rooting for you

Hey black man, hey black man, yes I'm talking to you

I love the poise that you possess, stomp the yard

Make a lot of noise

Make it clear you're here to demand your respect

Because you are a force to be reckoned with

Hey black man, hey black man, yea, I'm talking to you

You're a good-looking man, your skin glows differently

Because it glows from within

Astonishingly and amazingly unapologetic

Hey black man, hey black man, yea, I'm talking to you

Your intelligence pours out of you like an overflowing river

The vibration from the dynamic words you speak

Roll off your tongue so graciously and courageously

The knowledge that you possess, the language you convey

Is a magnitude of the power that lives inside of you

Hey black man, hey black man, yea, I'm talking to you

Walk your walk, talk your talk, let the world know

That you are a black man of excellence, charm,

self-confidence, brilliance, hard work,

And you're extraordinairy, not to mention a man of integrity

Watch out now, a black man has arrived

And demands some appreciation

Hey black man, hey black man, yea, I'm talking to you

6/24/2020

I Can't Breathe

I can't breathe

As the knee of racial inequality pressed against me

I can't breathe

As the knee of poverty and the spirit of black hate

Pressed against me

I can't breathe

As the knee of bigotry, the secret KKK

Pressed against me

I can't breathe

As the knee of injustice, stereotype, prejudice,

And crooked cops

Pressed against me

I can't breathe

As the knee of the system that locks

My black brothers and sisters up

Because they look differently

Pressed against me

I can't breathe

As the knee of the system taking our children

Corrupts them, feeding them lies and self-hate

Pressed against me

I can't breathe

As the knee of religious discrimination and abomination

Pressed against me

I can't breathe

As the knee of the educational system

Folds right in front of me or lack thereof

Pressed against me

I can't breathe

As the knee of racism still being alive and well

Pressed against me

I can't breathe

As the knee of everything my mama taught me

Did not save me that day

Pressed against me

I can't breathe

As the knee of separation, humiliation, incarceration

And the tactics to intimidate

Pressed against me

As my breath leaves my body

My sight disappears, it goes dark

The noise in my ears gets quiet

And the blood stops flowing

I can't breathe

You have to breathe for me

You have to stand up for me

You have to fight for me

Don't let the same knee that silenced me, silence you

Breathe my black mother

Breathe my black father

Breathe my black sister

Breathe my black brother

Breathe my black son

Breathe my black daughter

Breathe my black grandmother and father

Aunts and uncles,

Breathe my black cousins, but most important

Breathe my black community

I can't breathe

Can you breathe for me?

6/24/2020

Unspoken Land

Take my hand, follow me to this unspoken land
Descend to now the unknowable
Descend to speak the unspeakable

Grab hold to the faith
The faith that demonstrates hope
The faith that demonstrates love
The faith that demonstrates freedom

Freedom from the bonds of unhappiness
Take the step towards life
Let your soul live, live for eternity
Place your trust in a Man that's almighty

Trust Him to fight your battles
Trust Him to protect you from your enemies
Stand still and watch God show up and show out
Stand still and watch God show you His will

Take my hand, follow me to this unspoken land
Where the gates will open

The sun will shine

There will be no more tears or worries

No more heartache or loneliness

All of this will come to an end

Just take my hand and follow me to this unspoken land

2/26/2011

It's Hard to Say Goodbye

It's hard to say goodbye

Every day it gets harder and I wish you were here

I know you're here in spirit and always in my heart

My tears are full of sadness

My heart is full of hurt

I know you're in a better place

But it's still so hard to say goodbye

My nights get darker

You're not here when I need someone to talk to

But I know that you are near me watching over me

People hurt me but I know they are only for a season

While you are forever

Saying goodbye was so hard

To look at your cold hard body without movement

I cried

I miss you so much

Why me? Why now? Why ever?

I think my heart and my soul began to sink

My joy had left, and my love became cold

I'm no longer whole

I miss you, come save me

Save me from this world we call life

It is killing me like a sharp knife

It's so hard to say goodbye to you

I feel so blue

I miss you

It's so hard to say goodbye

July 2012

About the Author

Born to drug-addicted parents, Mishon Moore is a native Detroiter who came from nothing yet is focused on having everything. She experienced the death of both parents before she really knew herself. A domestic abuse and sexual assault survivor, Mishon is determined not to be a product of the circumstances she was born into. She is now a mother, college graduate, and entrepreneur who is allowing her voice to be heard through her poetry.

www.ingramcontent.com/pod-product-compliance
Lightning Source LLC
Chambersburg PA
CBHW071408070526
44578CB00002B/525